English-Chinese Terminology Handbook for Nurses

Key English-Chinese-English Terms for Healthcare Professionals

英语—中文

中文—英语

José Luis Leyva - Wei Wong

PREFACE

This book will be a valuable resource for nurses and other healthcare professionals who deal with Chinese speaking patients. It is a guide that contains the key and most frequently used healthcare terms. It will also be useful for Chinese speaking nurses who want to have a better communication while interacting with English speaking healthcare professionals.

ENGLISH-CHINESE
英语—中文

A

abdomen, 腹部

abdominal, 腹部的

abnormal, 异常

abortion, 流产

abrasion, 擦伤

abscess, 脓肿

abstinence, 禁戒

abuse, 滥用

accident, 事故

acetaminophen, 醋胺酚

ache, 疼痛

acid, 酸

acne, 痤疮

active, 主动的

acute, 急性的

addict, 成瘾

addiction, 成瘾性

admit (into hospital), 入（院）

adolescence, 青春期

adopt (to), 采（用）

adult, 成人

adrenaline, 肾上腺素

advise (to), 建议（进行）

afterbirth, 胞衣

agitation, 搅拌

ailment, 小病

air, 空气

alcoholism, 酒精中毒

alive, 活着

allergic, 过敏的

allergy, 过敏

ambulance, 救护车

amenorrhea, 闭经

amino acid, 氨基酸

ammonia, 氨

amnesia, 失忆

amniocentesis, 羊膜穿刺术

amniotic sac, 羊膜囊

amphetamines, 安非他明

amputate (to), 截肢 （以便）

amyotrophic lateral sclerosis, 肌萎缩性脊髓侧索硬化症

analgesic, 止痛药

analysis, 分析

anaphylactic, 过敏性的

anatomy, 解剖

anemia, 贫血

anemic, 贫血的

anesthesia, 麻醉

anesthesiologist, 麻醉师

aneurysm/aneurism, 动脉瘤

anger, 愤怒

angiogram, 血管造影

angioplasty, 血管成形术

anorexia, 厌食

antacid, 抗酸剂

anthrax, 炭疽

antibiotic, 抗生素

antibodies, 抗体

anticoagulant, 抗凝剂

antidepressant, 抗抑郁药

antidote, 解毒药

antihistamine, 抗组胺药

anus, 肛门

anxiety, 焦虑

aorta, 主动脉

apathy, 冷淡

apnea, 呼吸暂停

appendectomy, 阑尾切除术

appendicitis, 阑尾炎

appetite, 食欲

applicator, 涂药器

appointment, 预约

arm, 手臂

arm pit, 腋窝

arrhythmia, 心律不齐

artery, 动脉

arthritis, 关节炎

asphyxia, 窒息

asthma, 哮喘

asthmatic, 哮喘的

astigmatism, 散光

athlete's foot, 脚癣

atrophy, 萎缩

autism, 自闭症

autopsy, 尸检

awake, 苏醒

awaken (to), 唤醒（以便）

B

baby, 宝宝

back, 后背

backbone, 脊椎

bacteria, 细菌

bad, 不良

balance, 平衡

bald, 秃头的

baldness, 秃头

bandage, 绷带

bandaid, 急救绷带

barbiturates, 巴比妥类药物

barium, 钡

basin, 盆

bath, 洗澡

bathe (to), 洗澡（以便）

bed, 床

bedpan, 便盆

bedridden (patient), 卧床不起（患者）

bed-wetting, 尿床

behavior, 行为

belch, 打嗝

belly, 肚子

bellybutton, 肚脐

benign, 良性的

bib, 围兜

biceps, 肱二头肌

bicuspid, 双尖牙

bile, 胆

bilirubin, 胆红素

biological, 生物的

biopsy, 活检

birth, 出生

birthmark, 胎记

bite, 咬伤

bite (insect), 咬伤（昆虫）

bitter, 苦味的

blackheads, 黑头

bladder, 膀胱

bleed, 出血

blind, 失明的

blindness, 失明

blink, 眨眼

blister, 脓疱

blockage, 堵塞

blood, 血液

body, 身体

bone, 骨骼

booster shot, 强化注射剂量

bottle, 瓶

botulism, 肉毒杆菌中毒

bowel, 肠

brace, 娇正架

braces (dental), 娇正架（牙齿）

brain, 大脑

break, 破裂

breast/chest, 乳房/胸部

breastbone, 胸骨

breath, 呼吸

breathe, 呼吸

broken, 破碎的

bronchitis, 支气管炎

bruise, 瘀伤

bruised, 有瘀伤的

bulimia, 贪食症

bulimic, 贪食的

bump, 肿块

bunion, 拇囊肿

burn, 烧伤

burp, 饱嗝

bursitis, 滑囊炎

buttock, 臀部

buzzing, 嗡嗡声

C

calcified, 钙化的

calcium, 钙

calf (of leg), 腓（小腿肚）

callus, 愈伤组织

calorie, 卡路里

cancer, 癌症

cancerous, 癌的

cane, 手杖

capillary, 毛心血管

capsule, 胶囊

carbohydrate, 碳水化合物

carcinogenic, 致癌的

carcinoma, 癌

cardiac, 心脏病的

cardiologist, 心脏病学家

cardiology, 心脏病学

care, 护理

cartilage, 软骨

cast, 铸模

castration, 阉割

cataract, 白内障

catatonic, 紧张型

catheter, 导管

catheterization, 导尿术

catheterize, 导尿

cause, 原因

cauterize, 烧灼

cervix, 子宫颈

chafe, 擦伤

checkup, 检查

cheek, 脸颊

chemical, 化学

chemotherapy, 化疗

chest, 胸部

chew, 咀嚼

chicken pox, 鸡痘

childbirth, 分娩

childhood, 童年

chills, 发冷

chin, 下巴

chiropractor, 脊椎指压治疗师

chlamydia, 衣原体

choke, 哽噎

cholera, 霍乱

cholesterol, 胆固醇

chronic, 慢性

cigarette, 香烟

circulation, 循环

circumcision, 包皮环割术

cirrhosis, 肝硬化

claustrophobia, 幽闭恐惧症

cleft palate, 腭裂

clinic, 诊所

clitoris, 阴蒂

clot, 血块

cocaine, 可卡因

coccyx, 尾骨

codeine, 可待因

cold, 冷

cold (illness), 着凉（疾病）

cold sores, 唇疱疹

colic, 疝痛

colitis, 结肠炎

collagen, 胶原蛋白

collarbone, 锁骨

colon, 结肠

colonoscopy, 结肠镜检查

color-blindness, 色盲

colostomy, 结肠造口术

coma, 昏迷

comatose, 昏迷的

comfortable, 舒适的

complaint, 主诉

complexion, 肤色

complication, 并发症

compress, 敷布

conceive, 怀孕

concussion, 结论

condom, 避孕套

confused, 混乱的

confusion, 混乱

congenital, 先天的

congested (to be), 充血的

congestion, 充血

conjunctiva, 结膜

conjunctivitis, 结膜炎

conscious, 有意识的

consciousness, 意识

consent, 同意

constipation, 便秘

contagious, 传染性的

contaminated, 被污染的

contraception, 避孕

contractions, 挛缩

contusion, 挫伤

convalescent, 康复期的

convulsion, 惊厥

corn (callus), 鸡眼 （胼胝）

coronary, 冠状动脉的

cortisone, 可的松

cough, 咳嗽

cough, 咳嗽

CPR, 心肺复苏术

crabs, 阴虱寄生病

cramp, 抽筋

cramps (menstrual), 痛性痉挛（经期的）

cranium, 颅骨

craving, 渴望

crawl, 爬行

crib, 婴儿床

cripple, 瘸子

crippled, 瘸的

critical, 危象的

Crohn's disease, 克罗恩病

cross-eyed, 内斜视的

croup, 哮吼

crutches, 拐杖

cry, 哭泣

CT scan, CT扫描

culture, 培养物

cure, 治愈

cut, 切口

cuticle, 表皮

cyst, 囊肿

cystic fibrosis, 囊性纤维化

D

daily, 每日一次的

dandruff, 头皮屑

danger, 危险因素

daze, 使晕眩

dead, 死亡的

deaf, 聋的

deaf-mute, 聋哑者

deafness, 耳聋

death, 死亡

deceased, 死者

decongestant, 减充血剂

defecate, 排便

defibrillation, 心脏除颤

defibrillator, 除颤器

deficiency, 缺乏

deformed, 畸形的

deformity, 畸形

dehydration, 脱水

delirious, 谵妄的

delirium, 谵妄

delivery (of a baby), （胎儿的）分娩

deltoids, 三角肌

dementia, 痴呆

dental, 牙齿的

dentist, 牙科医生

denture, 假牙

depigmentation, 色素减退

depression, 抑郁症

dermatitis, 皮炎

dermatologist, 皮肤科医师

deterioration, 衰退

detoxification, 戒毒治疗

develop, 患(病)

diabetes, 糖尿病

diagnose, 诊断

diagnosis, 诊断

dialysis, 透析

diaper, 尿布

diaphragm, 横隔膜

diarrhea, 腹泻

die, 死亡

diet, 饮食

dietitian, 营养学家

digest, 消化

digestion, 消化系统

dilated, 扩张的

dilation, 扩张术

dilute, 稀释

diphtheria, 白喉

disability, 残疾

discharge, 排出

discharge from hospital, 出院

discontinue, 终止

disease, 疾病

disinfect, 消毒

disinfectant, 消毒剂

disk (slipped), 板 （滑脱）

dislocation, 脱臼

disorder, 紊乱

disorientation, 定向障碍

distend, 肿胀

distressed, 痛苦的

diuretic, 利尿剂

dizziness, 眩晕

dizzy, 眩晕的

doctor, 医生

doctor's office, 医师办公室

donor, 供体

dosage, 剂量

double vision, 复视

drain, 引流

draw blood, 使流血

dropper, 滴管

drops, 滴剂

drowning, 溺水

drowsy, 困倦的

drug addiction, 药物依赖

drugs (usually illicit), 毒品（通常是非法的）

drugs (legal), 麻醉药（合法的）

drunk, 酗酒者

dryness, 干燥

due date, 到期日

dull (pain), 迟钝的（疼痛）

duodenum, 十二指肠

dust, 尸体

dwarfism, 侏儒症

dysentery, 痢疾

dyslexia, 诵读困难

dystrophy, 营养不良

.

E

ear (inner), 耳（内）

ear (middle), 耳（中）

ear (outer), 耳（外）

earache, 耳痛

eardrum, 鼓膜

earlobe, 耳垂

earplugs, 耳塞

eczema, 湿疹

edema, 水肿

egg, 卵母细胞

ejaculate, 射出

EKG, 心电图

elbow, 肘

elderly, 年长的

electrocardiogram, 心电图

electrocution, 电处死

elixir, 酏剂

emaciated, 衰弱的

embolism, 栓塞

embryo, 胚胎

emergency, 急诊

pulmonary emphysema, 肺气肿

encephalitis, 脑炎

endemic, 地方病

endocrine, 内分泌的

endocrinologist, 内分泌学家

endorphin, 内啡肽

endoscopy, 内窥镜检查

enema, 灌肠剂

enlargement, 膨大

enzyme, 酶

epidemic, 流行病

epidural, 硬膜外的

epiglottis, 会厌

epilepsy, 癫痫

erection, 勃起

esophagus, 食管

estrogen, 雌激素

ether, 乙醚

euphoria, 欣快

Eustachian tube, 咽鼓管

euthanasia, 安乐死

exam, 体检

examine, 诊察

excrement, 排泄物

exercise, 锻炼

exertion, 劳累

exfoliation, 去角质化

exhale, 呼气

exhaustion, 衰竭

expectorant, 祛痰作用

expert, 专家

explain, 解释

exposure, 暴露

external, 外部

extract, 提取物

extraction, 萃取

eye, 眼睛

eyebrow, 眉毛

eyelash, 睫毛

eyelid, 眼睑

eyesight, 视力

F

face, 脸

face down, 脸朝下

face up, 脸朝上

faint, 微弱

fainting spells, 眩晕症

fall, 跌倒

Fallopian tubes, 输卵管

false teeth, 假牙

family planning, 计划生育

fast, 快速

fat (food), 脂肪 (食物)

fat (person), 脂肪 (人体)

fatal, 致命

fatigue, 疲劳

fear, 恐惧

feces, 粪便

feed, 进食

feel, 感觉

feet, 双脚

femur, 股骨

fertile, 多产

fertilization, 受精

fetal monitor, 胎儿监护仪

fetus, 胎儿

fever, 发烧

fiber, 纤维

fibrillation, 颤动

filling (dental), 填料（牙科）

finger, 手指

finger pad, 手指垫

fire, 火

first aid, 急救

fissure, 裂隙

fist, 拳头

flake, 片状

flat foot, 平足

flatulence, 胃肠胀气

flexible, 灵活

flu, 流感

fluoride, 氟化物

flush, 冲刷

foam, 泡沫

folic acid, 叶酸

folk healer, 江湖郎中

follicle, 菁荚果

follow-up, 后续

food, 食品

foot, 脚

forceps, 产钳

forearm, 前臂

forehead, 额头

foreskin, 包皮

form, 表格

formula, 奶粉

fracture, 骨折

freckle, 祛斑

freeze, 冻结

frequency, 频率

fright, 惊吓

function, 功能

fungus, 真菌

G

gag, 吞咽

gain weight, 增加体重

gall bladder, 胆囊

gallstones, 胆结石

gangrene, 坏疽

gargle, 含漱液

gas, 气体

gash, 口子

gastric ulcer, 胃溃疡

gastritis, 胃炎

gastroenterologist, 胃肠病学家

gastrointestinal (GI), 胃肠道 (GI)

gauze, 纱布

gel, 凝胶

gender, 性别

genes, 基因

genetic, 遗传

genitals, 生殖器官

geriatric, 老年医学

germ, 胚芽

German measles, 德国麻疹

gestation, 妊娠

gigantism, 巨人症

giardia, 贾第鞭毛虫

gingivitis, 牙龈炎

gland, 腺

glasses, 眼镜

glaucoma, 青光眼

glove, 手套

glucose, 葡萄糖

gluten, 面筋

goiter, 甲状腺肿大

gonorrhea, 淋病

goose bumps, 鸡皮疙瘩

gout, 痛风

gown, 患者服

graft, 移植物

gram, 克

grief, 悲伤

grieve, 悲伤

grind, 磨碎

groin, 腹股沟

growth, 增长

guilt, 内疚

gums, 牙龈

gun, 枪

gurney, 轮床

gut, 肠道

gynecologist, 妇科医生

gynecology, 妇科

H

habit, 习惯

hair, 头发

hair (body), 毛发 (人体)

halitosis, 口臭

hallucination, 幻觉

hammer, 锤子

hamstring, 腿筋

hand, 手

hangnail, 刺

hangover, 残留物

hardening, 硬化

harm, 伤害，损伤

harmful, 有害的

harmless, 无害的

head, 头部

headache, 头痛

heal, 治愈

health, 健康

health care, 卫生保健

healthy, 健康的

hear, 听到

hearing, 听力

heart, 心脏

heart attack, 心脏病发作

heartbeat, 心跳

heartburn, 胃灼热

heat-stroke, 中暑

heating pad, 加热垫

heel, 脚后跟，踵

height, 高度，身高

helicopter, 直升机

hematoma, 血肿

hemoglobin, 血红素

hemophilia, 血友病

hemorrhage, 出血

hepatitis, 肝炎

herb, 草药

herbalist, 草药医生

hereditary, 遗传的

heredity, 遗传

hermaphrodite, 具有两性者；两性体；阴阳人

hernia, 疝气；脱肠

heroin, 海洛因

herpes, 疱疹

heterosexual, 异性的

hiccups, 呃逆

high blood pressure, 高血压

hip, 臀部

hives, 荨麻疹

hoarse, 声嘶的

hoarseness, 声嘶

homeopathy, 顺势疗法

homosexual, 同性恋爱的

hookworm, 钩虫；十二指肠虫；十二指肠病

hormonal, 荷尔蒙的

hormone, 荷尔蒙，激素

hospital, 医院

hospitalize, 入院治疗

hot flashes, 潮热

hunchback, 驼背

hurt, 疼痛

hydrate, 水合物；氢氧化物

hydrogen peroxide, 过氧化氢

hygiene, 卫生保健学

hymen, 处女膜

hyperactive, 极度亢奋的

hyperglycemia, 血糖过高症

hypersensitivity, 过敏症

hypertension, 高血压

hyperthermia, 过高热

hyperthyroidism, 甲状腺机能亢进

hyperventilation, 换气过度，强力呼吸

hypochondria, 忧郁症，臆想病

hypoglycemia, 血糖过低；低血糖症

hypothalamus, 丘脑下部

hypothermia, 降低体温

hypothyroidism, 甲状腺机能减退

hypoxia, 组织缺氧；氧不足

hysterectomy, 子宫切除

hysteria, 癔病

I

ibuprofen, 布洛芬（一种退烧和解除疼痛的止痛药）

ill, 疾病

illness, 疾病；生病

immature, 未成熟的，未发育完全的

immobile, 固定的

immobilization, 制动术

immune, 免疫的

immunize, 使免疫，赋予免疫性

impacted tooth, 阻生齿

impaired, 损害

impairment, 损害；损伤

implant, 嵌入，灌输，植入

impotence, 阳萎

impregnation, 受孕，受精，浸渗作用

incest, 血亲相奸，乱伦

incision, 切口

incontinence, 失禁

incubator, 早产儿保育器

incurable, 无法治愈的

indigestion, 消化不良

induce, 诱导，感应

infant, 婴幼儿

infect, 传染；感染

infection, 传染病；传染，传播，感染

infertile, 不能生育的

infertility, 不育

inflammation, 炎症

influenza, 流行性感冒

ingest, 摄取；吸收

inhale, 吸入

inhaler, 吸入器

inject, 注射

injury, 伤，损伤

inoculate, 接种

inoculation, 疫苗接种

insane, 患精神病的

insanity, 精神失常；精神错乱

insemination, 授精；怀孕

insomnia, 不眠症

instrument, 仪器，器械

insulin, 胰岛素

insurance, 保险

intensive care, 重病特别护理

intercourse, 性交行为

internal, 内部器官，内脏

internist, 内科医师

intestine, 肠

intoxication, 中毒，毒化，腐蚀

intravenous fluids, 静脉输液

intubation, 插管，插管法

iodine, 碘，碘酒

iron, 铁

irregular heartbeat, 心律不齐

irrigate, 冲洗伤口

irritation, 刺激作用，兴奋

itch, 痒，痒病

J

jaundice, 黄疸

jaw, 颚；下巴；颌

jelly, 凝胶，胶冻

jock itch, 股癣

joint, 关节

jugular, 咽喉的，颈静脉的

juice, 汁，液

K

kidney, 肾脏

kidney failure, 肾功能衰竭

kidney stones, 肾结石

knee, 膝盖

kneecap, 膝盖骨

knife, 刀，手术刀

knot, 节疤

knuckle, 指关节

L

labor, 分娩

labor pains, 分娩阵痛

laboratory, 实验室

labyrinthitis, 内耳炎

laceration, 撕裂伤

lactation, 哺乳

lactose, 乳糖

lame extremity, 跛行

language, 语言

laparoscopy, 腹腔镜检查

large intestine, 大肠

laryngitis, 喉炎

larynx, 咽喉

laser treatment, 激光疗法

latex, 乳胶

laughing gas, 笑气

laxative, 泻药

lead, 导联/导线/电极

leech, 水蛭

left-handed, 用左手的/左撇子

leg, 腿部

leprosy, 麻风病

lesbian, 女同性恋

lesion, 病灶

lethargy, 昏睡/嗜眠症

leukemia, 白血病

libido, 性欲

lice, 虱子

life, 生命/生活

lifestyle, 生活方式

ligament, 韧带

light-headedness, 头晕目眩

limb, 肢

liniment, 搽剂

liposuction, 抽脂术

lips, 嘴唇

liquid, 液体

lisp, 口齿不清

listen, 倾听

live, 活的/精力充沛的

liver, 肝脏

lobe, （肺、脑等）叶

lobotomy, 脑叶切除术

lockjaw, 牙关紧闭症

low blood pressure, 低血压

lozenges, 锭剂

lubricate, 润滑

lump, 肿块

lumpectomy, 肿块切除术

lungs, 肺

lupus, 狼疮

lymph, 淋巴

lymph nodes, 淋巴结

lymphoma, 淋巴瘤

M

malabsorption, 吸收不良

malaise, 不适

malaria, 疟疾

male, 男性/雄性

malformation, 畸形

malignant, 恶性的

malnutrition, 营养不良

malpractice, 治疗不当

mammogram, 乳房X光片

mania, 躁狂

manic-depressive, 躁郁症

marijuana, 大麻

mask, 面罩

mass, 团块

massage/rub, 按摩/揉

mastectomy, 乳房切除术

maternal, 母性/母体

maturity, 成熟期/发育成熟

measles, 麻疹

medical record, 病历

medication, 药物/药物治疗

medicine, 药品/医药

melanoma, 黑素瘤

meningitis, 脑膜炎

menopause, 更年期

menses, 月经

menstrual cycle, 月经周期

menstruation, 月经

mental illness, 精神疾病

metabolism, 新陈代谢

metastasis, 转移病变/扩散

methadone, 美沙酮

methamphetamine, 甲基苯丙胺

microscope, 显微镜

microsurgery, 显微外科

midwife, 助产士

migraine, 偏头痛

mind, 精神/头脑/心理

miscarriage, 流产

mite, 螨

mole, 痣

monitor, 监护仪/监查员

mononucleosis, 单核细胞增多症

morgue, 太平间/停尸房

morphine, 咖啡

mortality, 死亡率

mouth, 口腔/嘴

mucous, 粘液

mumps, 腮腺炎

muscle, 肌肉

mutation, 突变

mute, 静音/哑

myopia, 近视

N

nail, 指甲

naked, 裸露的

nap, 小睡

nape, 颈背

narcolepsy, 发作性嗜睡病

narcotic, 麻醉药/麻醉性

natural, 自然/天然/固有

nausea, 恶心

navel, 肚脐

nearsightedness, 近视眼

neck, 颈部

needle, 穿刺针/针头

nerve, 神经

nervous, 神经性/紧张

neuralgia, 神经痛

neurologist, 神经病学家

neurology, 神经学/神经科

neurosis, 神经官能症

neurotic, 神经病患者

nicotine, 尼古丁

nightmare, 恶梦

nipple, 乳头

nitroglycerine, 硝酸甘油

normal, 正常/常态

nose, 鼻

nostril, 鼻孔

nourishment, 营养

numbness, 麻木

nurse, 护士

nutrient, 营养物/营养的

nutrition, 营养品/营养作用/营养/营养学

nutritionist, 营养学家

O

obese, 肥胖

obesity, 肥胖症

obstetrician, 产科医生

obstetrics, 产科

obstruction, 梗阻

occlusion, 闭塞

odor, 恶臭

office, 办公室

ointment, 软膏

oncologist, 肿瘤科医生

oncology, 肿瘤学

operate, 操作

ophthalmologist, 眼科医生

optic, 光

optometrist, 验光师

oral, 口

organ, 器官

orgasm, 性高潮

orthodontist, 正牙医生

orthopedics, 骨科

orthopedist, 骨科医生

osteoarthritis, 矫形外科医生

osteopath, 骨关节炎

osteoporosis, 骨质疏松症

ovary, 卵巢

overdose, 过量

overweight, 超重

ovulate, 排卵

ovulation, 排卵期

oxygen, 氧

P

pacemaker, 起搏器

pacifier, 橡皮奶头

pain, 疼痛

pain reliever, 止痛药

painful, 疼痛的

palate, 腭

pale, 苍白

paleness, 苍白

palpitations, 心悸

pancreas, 胰腺

Pap smear, 巴氏涂片

paralysis, 麻痹

paralyzed, 瘫痪

paramedic, 护理人员

paranoia, 偏执

paraplegic, 截瘫

parasite, 寄生虫

patch, 斑块

paternal, 父本

pathologist, 病理医生

patient, 患者

pediatric, 儿科

pediatrician, 儿科医师

pediatrics, 儿科

pelvis, 骨盘

penetrate, 渗透

penicillin, 青霉素

penis, 阴茎

perforation, 穿孔

perspire, 出汗

pertussis, 百日咳

pharmacist, 药师

pharmacy, 药学

pharynx, 咽

phlegm, 痰

phobia, 恐怖症

phosphorus, 磷

photosensitivity, 光敏性

physical therapy, 理疗

physician, 医生

pill, 药片

pillow, 枕

pimples, 暗疮

placenta, 胎盘

plague, 鼠疫

plaque, 斑块

plasma, 血浆

platelets, 血小板

pneumonia, 肺炎

podiatrist, 足医

poison, 毒物

polio, 脊髓灰质炎

pollen, 花粉

polyp, 息肉

pore, 孔

postmenopausal, 绝经后

post-op, 术后

postpartum, 产后

potassium, 钾

pound, 磅

powder, 粉剂

predispose, 先兆

preeclampsia, 先兆子痫

pregnancy, 妊娠

pregnant, 妊娠

premature birth, 早产

premenopausal, 绝经前

prenatal care, 产前保健

prescribe, 开处方

prescription, 处方

pressure, 压力

prevent, 预防

prevention, 预防

procedure, 程序

proctologist, 肛肠科医生

progesterone, 孕酮

prognosis, 预后

prostate gland, 前列腺

protein, 蛋白

psoriasis, 银屑病

psychiatrist, 精神科医生

psychologist, 心理医生

psychosis, 精神病

psychotherapy, 心理治疗

psychotic, 精神病性

puberty, 青春期

pubic hair, 阴毛

pulmonary, 肺

pulmonary edema, 肺水肿

pulsating, 脉动

pulse, 脉搏

pump, 泵

pupil, 瞳孔

pus, 脓

Q

quadriceps, 股四头肌

quarantine, 检疫

quinine, 奎宁

quota, 指标

R

rabies, 狂犬病

radiation treatment, 放疗

radiologist, 放射科医生

radiology, 放射学

radiotherapy, 放疗

rape, 强奸

rash, 皮疹

reaction, 反应

reconstruct, 重建

recovery, 恢复

rectum, 直肠

redness, 发红，红斑

refill, 再装（或注、填）满、补加(处方)

reflex, 反射

reflux, 回流

regurgitation, 回流、关闭不全

rehabilitate, 康复

rehydrate, 再水化、补充水分

reject, 拒绝、排斥、吐出或呕吐

relapse, 复发

relationship (family), 关系（家庭）

relax, 放松、缓和、减轻、（使大便等）通畅

relief, (痛苦等的)缓和、减轻

remedy, 治疗

renal failure, 肾功能衰竭

replace, 更换、替代

reproduce, 生殖、繁殖

reproduction, 生殖、繁殖

respirator, 呼吸器

respiratory, 呼吸的

rest, 休息

result, 结果

resuscitation, 复苏

retention, 潴留、保留、滞留

retina, 视网膜

revive, 复活、复苏

rheumatic fever, 风湿热

rheumatism, 风湿病

rhinoplasty, 隆鼻

rhythm method, 安全期避孕法

rib, 肋骨

rigidity, 强直,僵硬

rigor mortis, 尸僵

risk, 风险

rubella, 风疹

runny nose, 流鼻涕

rupture, 破裂

S

safe, 安全的

saline, 盐水

saliva, 口水

salmonella, 沙门氏菌

salt, 盐

sample, 样本

sane, 神志正常的

sanitary, 卫生

sanity, 神志正常

sarcoma, 肉瘤

scab, 结痂、痂

scabies, 疥疮

scald, 烫伤

scale, 规模、天平、鳞屑、鳞片

scalp, 头皮

scaly, 鳞片状

scar, 疤痕

scarlet fever, 猩红热

schizophrenia, 精神分裂症

sciatica, 坐骨神经痛

scissors, 剪刀

scoliosis, 脊柱侧凸

scratch, 擦伤、搔痒

scream, 尖叫

screen, 屏幕、筛选

scrotum, 阴囊

scurvy, 坏血病

sealant, 密封剂

seasickness, 晕船

secrete, 分泌

secretion, 分泌、分泌物

sedative, 镇静的、镇静剂

sedentary, 久坐不动、坐式的

seizures, 癫痫发作、突然发作

semen, 精液

senile, 老年的、衰老的

senility, 衰老

sensation, 感觉

sensitive, 敏感的

sensitivity, 敏感、灵敏度

septum, 隔膜

serious, 严重的

serum, 血清

severe, 严重的、剧烈的

sex, 性别

sexuality, 性欲

shakes, 颤抖

sharp (pain), 剧烈的（疼痛）

shin, 胫骨

shingles, 带状疱疹

shiver, 哆嗦战栗

shiver, 哆嗦、战栗

shock, 休克

shot, (疫苗等的)注射、(麻醉剂等的)一次注射

shoulder, 肩

shoulder blade, 肩胛骨

sibling, 兄弟姐妹

sick, 生病的

sickness, 疾病

side, 侧面、侧面的、边、面

side effect, 副作用

sight, 视力

sinus, 窦

sinusitis, 鼻窦炎

skeleton, 骨架

skin, 皮肤

skinny, 瘦

skull, 颅骨

sleep, 睡眠、睡觉

sleeping pill, 安眠药

sleepy, 困的

sling, 悬带

slip, 滑 、（健康状况等）变差

slipped disc, 椎间盘突出

sliver, 银

slur, 含糊地发音

small intestine, 小肠

smallpox, 天花

smell, 闻 、气味

smoke, 烟、吸烟

snakebite, （尤指毒蛇咬的）蛇咬伤

sneeze, 打喷嚏

snore, 打鼾

soap, 肥皂

sober, 清醒的

social worker, 社会工作者

sodium, 钠

sole (of foot), （脚的）脚底

sonogram, 超声波图

sore, 痛、疼痛的

spasm, 痉挛、抽搐

specialist, 专家、专科医生

specimen, 标本、（化验的）抽样

speculum, 诊视器、窥镜

speech pathologist, 语言病理学家

sperm, 精子

spermicide, 杀精剂

sphincter, 括约肌

spider bite, 蜘蛛咬伤

spina bifida, 脊柱裂

spinal column, 脊柱

spinal cord, 脊髓

spleen, 脾

splint (n), （用于固定断骨等的）夹板（名词）

splint (v), 用夹板固定（断肢等）（动词）

splinter, 碎片

sponge, 海绵

spots, 斑点

spotted fever, 斑疹热

sprain, 扭伤

sputum, 痰

stab, 刺伤

stain, 染色

starvation, 饥饿

sterile, 无菌的

sterility, 不育；无菌

sterilize, 消毒

sternum, 胸骨

steroid, 类固醇

stethoscope, 听诊器

stiff, 僵硬

stimulant, 刺激物

sting, 叮，刺

sting, 刺

stirrup, 马镫

stitches, 缝线；缝针

stoma, 人造口；小孔

stomach, 胃

stomach ache/pain, 胃痛/痛

stool, 大便

strangle, 窒息而死

strength, 力量

strep, 链球菌

stress, 压力

stretch mark, 妊娠纹，白纹

stretcher, 担架

stroke, 卒中

strong, 强壮; 强

stuffy nose, 鼻塞

stupor, 昏迷

stutter, 口吃

suffocation, 窒息

suicide, 自杀

sunburn, 晒伤

sunstroke, 中暑

suppository, 栓剂

surgeon, 外科医生

surgery, 手术

surrogate mother, 代孕母亲

survive, 生存

suture, 缝合

swab, 拭子；医用海绵，纱布

swallow, 咽下

sweat, 汗液

swelling, 肿胀

swollen, 肿

symptom, 症状

syndrome, 综合征

synthetic, 合成

syphilis, 梅毒

syringe, 注射器

syrup, 糖浆

T

table, (头颅的)骨板

tablespoonful, 一汤匙量

tablet, 片剂；药片

tailbone, 尾骨

take, 取；服药

talcum powder, 滑石粉；爽身粉

tampon, 卫生棉条；止血塞

tapeworm, 绦虫

taste, 味道；味觉

taste bud, 味蕾

tattoo, 纹身

tear (of muscle/ligament), （肌肉/韧带）撕裂

tear (of the eye), （眼）泪

teaspoonful, 一茶匙的量

technician, 技术员

temperature, 温度

temple (of the head), 太阳穴；颞颥；鬓角

temporary, 临时

tender, 温柔的；柔软的；

tendinitis, 肌腱炎

tendon, 肌腱

terminal, 末端的

test, 测试

testicles, 睾丸

testosterone, 睾酮

tetanus, 破伤风；强直

therapist, 治疗师

therapy, 治疗

thermometer, 温度计

thick, 厚

thigh, 大腿

thirst, 口渴

thirsty (to be), 渴望（成为）

thorax, 胸部

throat, 喉咙

throbbing, 悸动；搏动

thrombosis, 血栓

throw up, 呕吐

thumb, 拇指

thyroid gland, 甲状腺

tincture, 酊剂

tingling, 刺痛

tinnitus, 耳鸣

tissue, 组织

tobacco, 烟草

toe, 脚趾

toilet, 厕所

tolerate, 容忍

tongue, 舌

tonic, 进补

tonsil, 扁桃体

tonsillectomy, 扁桃体切除术

tonsillitis, 扁桃体炎

tooth, 牙齿

toothache, 牙痛

touch, 触摸

tourniquet, 止血带

towel, 毛巾

toxemia, 毒血症

toxic, 有毒

toxin, 毒素

trace, 跟踪

trachea, 气管

traction, 牵引

tranquilizers, 镇静剂

transfusion, 输血

transmitted, 传播

transplant, 移植

trauma, 创伤

traumatic, 外伤性

treat, 治疗（动词）

treatment, 治疗

tremors, 震颤

triceps, 三头肌

trouble, 麻烦

tube, 管

tuberculosis, 肺结核

tumor, 肿瘤

tweezers, 镊子；小钳子

twin, 双胞胎

twisted, 扭曲的；變形的

typhoid fever, 傷寒

typhus, 斑疹傷寒

U

ulcer, 潰瘍

ultrasound, 超音波

umbilical cord, 臍帶

uncomfortable, 不舒服

unconscious, 意識不清

unhealthy, 不健康

unstable, 不穩定

urethra, 尿道

urgent, 緊急

urinal, 尿道

urinalysis, 尿液分析

urinary, 尿液的、 泌尿系統的

urinate, 排尿

urine, 尿液

urine sample, 尿液檢體

urologist, 泌尿科醫師

urology, 泌尿科學

uterus, 子宮

V

vaccinate, 接種疫苗

vaccine, 疫苗

vagina, 陰道

vaginal, 陰道的

vaginitis, 陰道炎

valve, 瓣膜(瓣)

varicose vein, 靜脈曲張

vascular, 血管的

vasectomy, 輸精管切除術

vegetative, 植物人狀態的

vein, 靜脈曲張

venereal disease, 性病

venom, (蛇、蜘蛛等)毒液

ventilator, 呼吸器

ventricle, 室、心室

vertebrae, 脊椎骨

vertigo, 眩暈

victim, 患者

virile, 有生殖力的

virus, 病毒

vision, 視力

visiting hours, 探病時間

vital, 生命的

vital organ, 重要器官

vital signs, 生命徵象

vitamin, 維他命、維生素

vocal cord, 聲帶

vomit, 嘔吐

W

waist, 腰部

waiting room, 候診室、等待室

wake up, 醒來

walker, 助行器

ward, 單位 (病房)

warning, 警告

wart, 疣

wash (to), 洗滌

water, 水

watery eyes, 淚漏

weak, 虛弱的

weakness, 虛弱

wean, 戒斷、戒除

weary, 疲倦

weigh, 称重

weight, 體重

weight change, 體重變化

wet nurse, 奶媽

wheel chair, 輪椅

wheeze, 哮鳴

wheeze, 哮鳴

white blood cells, 白血球

whooping cough (pertussis), 百日咳

windpipe, 氣管

wisdom tooth, 智齒

womb, 子宮

worms (intestinal), 蛔蟲

wound, 傷口

wrist, 手腕

X

x-rays, X光

Y

yawn, 打哈欠

CHINESE-ENGLISH
中文—英语

CT扫描, CT scan

X光, x-rays

一汤匙量, tablespoonful

一茶匙的量, teaspoonful

三头肌 , triceps

三角肌, deltoids

下巴, chin

不健康, unhealthy

不眠症, insomnia

不穩定, unstable

不育, infertility

不育；无菌, sterility

不能生育的, infertile

不舒服, uncomfortable

不良, bad

不适, malaise

专家, expert

专家 、专科医生, specialist

丘脑下部, hypothalamus

严重的 , serious

严重的、剧烈的 , severe

中暑, heat-stroke

中暑 , sunstroke

中毒，毒化，腐蚀, intoxication

临时 , temporary

主动的, active

主动脉, aorta

主诉, complaint

久坐不动、坐式的 , sedentary

乙醚, ether

习惯, habit

乳头, nipple

乳房/胸部, breast/chest

乳房X光片, mammogram

乳房切除术, mastectomy

乳糖, lactose

乳胶, latex

事故, accident

产前保健, prenatal care

产后, postpartum

产科, obstetrics

产科医生, obstetrician

产钳, forceps

人造口 ; 小孔, stoma

代孕母亲, surrogate mother

仪器，器械, instrument

休克, shock

休息 , rest

会厌, epiglottis

传播, transmitted

传染；**感染**, infect

传染性的, contagious

传染病；传染，传播，感染, infection

伤，损伤, injury

伤害，损伤, harm

低血压, low blood pressure

体检, exam

使免疫，赋予免疫性, immunize

使晕眩, daze

使流血, draw blood

侏儒症, dwarfism

供体, donor

侧面、侧面的、边、面, side

便盆, bedpan

便秘, constipation

保险, insurance

候诊室、等待室, waiting room

倾听, listen

假牙, denture

假牙, false teeth

偏头痛, migraine

偏执, paranoia

健康, health

健康的, healthy

伤口, wound

伤寒, typhoid fever

僵硬 , stiff

儿科, pediatric

儿科, pediatrics

儿科医师, pediatrician

兄弟姐妹 , sibling

充血, congestion

充血的, congested (to be)

先兆, predispose

先兆子痫, preeclampsia

先天的, congenital

光, optic

光敏性, photosensitivity

克, gram

克罗恩病, Crohn's disease

免疫的, immune

入（院）, admit (into hospital)

入院治疗, hospitalize

关系（家庭）, relationship (family)

关节, joint

关节炎, arthritis

具有两性者；两性体；阴阳人, hermaphrodite

内分泌学家, endocrinologist

内分泌的, endocrine

内啡肽, endorphin

内斜视的, cross-eyed

内疚, guilt

内科医师, internist

内窥镜检查, endoscopy

内耳炎, labyrinthitis

内部器官，内脏, internal

再水化、补充水分, rehydrate

再装（或注、填）满、补加(处方), refill

冠状动脉的, coronary

冲刷, flush

冲洗伤口, irrigate

冷, cold

冷淡, apathy

冻结, freeze

减充血剂, decongestant

凝胶, gel

凝胶，胶冻, jelly

出汗, perspire

出生 , birth

出血, bleed

出血, hemorrhage

出院, discharge from hospital

刀，手术刀, knife

分娩, childbirth

分娩, labor

分娩 （胎儿的）, delivery (of a baby)

分娩阵痛, labor pains

分析, analysis

分泌 , secrete

分泌、分泌物 , secretion

切口, cut

切口, incision

创伤 , trauma

利尿剂, diuretic

到期日, due date

制动术, immobilization

刺, hangnail

刺 , sting

刺伤, stab

刺激作用，兴奋, irritation

刺激物, stimulant

刺痛 , tingling

剂量, dosage

前列腺, prostate gland

前臂, forearm

剧烈的（疼痛）, sharp (pain)

剪刀 , scissors

副作用 , side effect

力量, strength

办公室, office

功能, function

加热垫, heating pad

动脉, artery

动脉瘤, aneurysm/aneurism

助产士, midwife

助行器, walker

劳累, exertion

勃起, erection

包皮, foreskin

包皮环割术, circumcision

化学, chemical

化疗, chemotherapy

医师办公室, doctor's office

医生, doctor

医生, physician

医院, hospital

十二指肠, duodenum

卒中, stroke

单核细胞增多症, mononucleosis

卡路里, calorie

卧床不起 （患者）, bedridden (patient)

卫生 , sanitary

卫生保健, health care

卫生保健学, hygiene

卫生棉条；止血塞, tampon

危象的, critical

危险因素, danger

卵巢, ovary

卵母细胞, egg

压力, pressure

压力 , stress

厌食, anorexia

厕所 , toilet

厚 , thick

原因, cause

去角质化, exfoliation

双尖牙, bicuspid

双胞胎, twin

双脚, feet

反射 , reflex

反应, reaction

发作性嗜睡病, narcolepsy

发冷, chills

发烧, fever

发红， 红斑, redness

取；服药 , take

受孕， 受精， 浸渗作用, impregnation

受精, fertilization

口, oral

口吃 , stutter

口子, gash

口水 , saliva

口渴, thirst

口腔/嘴, mouth

口臭, halitosis

口齿不清, lisp

叮， 刺 , sting

可卡因, cocaine

可待因, codeine

可的松, cortisone

叶 （肺、脑等）, lobe

叶酸, folic acid

合成, synthetic

同性恋爱的, homosexual

同意, consent

后续, follow-up

后背, back

吞咽, gag

含漱液, gargle

含糊地发音, slur

听到, hear

听力, hearing

听诊器 , stethoscope

吸入, inhale

吸入器, inhaler

吸收不良, malabsorption

呃逆, hiccups

呕吐, throw up

味蕾 , taste bud

味道 ; 味觉, taste

呼吸, breath

呼吸, breathe

呼吸器, ventilator

呼吸器 , respirator

呼吸暂停, apnea

呼吸的 , respiratory

呼气, exhale

咀嚼, chew

咖啡, morphine

咬伤, bite

咬伤（昆虫）, bite (insect)

咳嗽, cough

咳嗽, cough

咽, pharynx

咽下, swallow

咽喉, larynx

咽喉的， 颈静脉的, jugular

咽鼓管, Eustachian tube

哆嗦 、战栗, shiver

哆嗦战栗, shiver

哭泣, cry

哮吼, croup

哮喘, asthma

哮喘的, asthmatic

哮鸣, wheeze

哮鸣, wheeze

哺乳, lactation

哽噎, choke

唇疱疹, cold sores

唤醒（以便）, awaken (to)

喉咙 , throat

喉炎, laryngitis

單位 (病房), ward

嗡嗡声, buzzing

呕吐, vomit

嘴唇, lips

器官, organ

囊性纤维化, cystic fibrosis

囊肿, cyst

回流 , reflux

回流、关闭不全 , regurgitation

团块, mass

困倦的, drowsy

困的, sleepy

围兜, bib

固定的, immobile

地方病, endemic

坏疽, gangrene

坏血病, scurvy

坐骨神经痛, sciatica

培养物, culture

基因, genes

堵塞, blockage

填料（牙科）, filling (dental)

增加体重, gain weight

增长, growth

声嘶, hoarseness

声嘶的, hoarse

处女膜, hymen

处方, prescription

复发, relapse

复活 、复苏, revive

复苏, resuscitation

复视, double vision

外伤性, traumatic

外科医生, surgeon

外部, external

多产, fertile

大便, stool

大肠, large intestine

大脑, brain

大腿, thigh

大麻, marijuana

天花, smallpox

太平间/停尸房, morgue

太阳穴；颞颥；鬓角, temple (of the head)

失忆, amnesia

失明, blindness

失明的, blind

失禁, incontinence

头发, hair

头晕目眩, light-headedness

头痛, headache

头皮, scalp

头皮屑, dandruff

头部, head

奎宁, quinine

女同性恋, lesbian

奶媽, wet nurse

奶粉, formula

妇科, gynecology

妇科医生, gynecologist

妊娠, gestation

妊娠, pregnancy

妊娠, pregnant

妊娠纹，白纹, stretch mark

娇正架, brace

娇正架（牙齿）, braces (dental)

婴儿床, crib

婴幼儿, infant

子宫切除, hysterectomy

子宫颈, cervix

子宫, uterus

子宫, womb

孔, pore

孕酮, progesterone

安乐死, euthanasia

安全期避孕法 , rhythm method

安全的 , safe

安眠药 , sleeping pill

安非他明, amphetamines

定向障碍, disorientation

宝宝, baby

实验室, laboratory

室、心室, ventricle

容忍, tolerate

寄生虫, parasite

密封剂, sealant

导尿, catheterize

导尿术, catheterization

导管, catheter

导联/导线/电极, lead

射出, ejaculate

小病, ailment

小睡, nap

小肠, small intestine

尖叫, scream

尸体, dust

尸僵, rigor mortis

尸检, autopsy

尼古丁, nicotine

尾骨, coccyx

尾骨, tailbone

尿布, diaper

尿床, bed-wetting

尿液, urine

尿液分析, urinalysis

尿液檢體, urine sample

尿液的、泌尿系統的, urinary

尿道, urethra

尿道, urinal

屏幕、筛选, screen

嵌入，灌输，植入, implant

巨人症, gigantism

巴比妥类药物, barbiturates

巴氏涂片, Pap smear

布洛芬（一种退烧和解除疼痛的止痛药）, ibuprofen

带状疱疹 , shingles

干燥, dryness

平衡, balance

平足, flat foot

年长的, elderly

并发症, complication

幻觉, hallucination

幽闭恐惧症, claustrophobia

床, bed

康复 , rehabilitate

康复期的, convalescent

建议（进行）, advise (to)

开处方, prescribe

异常, abnormal

异性的, heterosexual

引流, drain

强化注射剂量, booster shot

强壮; 强 , strong

强奸, rape

强直,僵硬, rigidity

循环, circulation

微弱, faint

德国麻疹, German measles

心律不齐, irregular heartbeat

心律不齐 , arrhythmia

心悸, palpitations

心理医生, psychologist

心理治疗, psychotherapy

心电图, EKG

心电图, electrocardiogram

心肺复苏术, CPR

心脏, heart

心脏病发作, heart attack

心脏病学, cardiology

心脏病学家, cardiologist

心脏病的, cardiac

心脏除颤, defibrillation

心跳, heartbeat

忧郁症，臆想病, hypochondria

快速, fast

怀孕, conceive

急性的, acute

急救, first aid

急救绷带, bandaid

急诊, emergency

性交行为, intercourse

性别, gender

性别 , sex

性欲, libido

性欲 , sexuality

性病, venereal disease

性高潮, orgasm

恐怖症, phobia

恐惧, fear

恢复 , recovery

息肉, polyp

恶心, nausea

恶性的, malignant

恶梦, nightmare

恶臭, odor

患(病), develop

患精神病的, insane

患者, patient

患者, victim

患者服, gown

悬带, sling

悲伤, grief

悲伤, grieve

悸动；搏动, throbbing

惊厥, convulsion

惊吓, fright

愈伤组织, callus

意識不清, unconscious

意识, consciousness

感觉, feel

感觉, sensation

愤怒, anger

慢性, chronic

成人, adult

成熟期/发育成熟, maturity

成瘾, addict

成瘾性, addiction

戒斷、戒除, wean

戒毒治疗, detoxification

截瘫, paraplegic

截肢（以便）, amputate (to)

扁桃体, tonsil

扁桃体切除术, tonsillectomy

扁桃体炎, tonsillitis

手, hand

手套, glove

手指, finger

手指垫, finger pad

手术, surgery

手杖, cane

手腕, wrist

手臂, arm

打哈欠, yawn

打喷嚏, sneeze

打嗝, belch

打鼾, snore

扩张术, dilation

扩张的, dilated

扭伤, sprain

扭曲的；變形的, twisted

技术员, technician

抑郁症, depression

抗体, antibodies

抗凝剂, anticoagulant

抗抑郁药, antidepressant

抗生素, antibiotic

抗组胺药, antihistamine

抗酸剂, antacid

护士, nurse

护理, care

护理人员, paramedic

抽筋, cramp

抽脂术, liposuction

担架 , stretcher

拇囊肿, bunion

拇指 , thumb

拐杖, crutches

拒绝、排斥、吐出或呕吐, reject

括约肌 , sphincter

拭子；医用海绵，纱布, swab

拳头, fist

指关节, knuckle

指标, quota

指甲, nail

按摩/揉, massage/rub

挛缩, contractions

挫伤, contusion

损害, impaired

损害；损伤, impairment

换气过度，强力呼吸, hyperventilation

授精；怀孕, insemination

排便, defecate

排出, discharge

排卵, ovulate

排卵期, ovulation

排尿, urinate

排泄物, excrement

探病時間, visiting hours

接种, inoculate

接種疫苗, vaccinate

提取物, extract

插管，插管法, intubation

搅拌, agitation

搽剂, liniment

摄取；吸收, ingest

撕裂（肌肉/韧带）, tear (of muscle/ligament)

撕裂伤, laceration

操作, operate

擦伤, abrasion

擦伤, chafe

擦伤、搔痒, scratch

支气管炎, bronchitis

放射学, radiology

放射科医生, radiologist

放松、 缓和、减轻、（使大便等）通畅, relax

放疗, radiation treatment

放疗, radiotherapy

敏感、灵敏度 , sensitivity

敏感的, sensitive

救护车, ambulance

散光, astigmatism

敷布, compress

斑块, patch

斑块, plaque

斑点, spots

斑疹伤寒, typhus

斑疹热 , spotted fever

新陈代谢, metabolism

无害的, harmless

无法治愈的, incurable

无菌的, sterile

早产, premature birth

早产儿保育器, incubator

昏睡/嗜眠症, lethargy

昏迷, coma

昏迷 , stupor

昏迷的, comatose

显微外科, microsurgery

显微镜, microscope

晒伤 , sunburn

晕船 , seasickness

智齿, wisdom tooth

暗疮, pimples

暴露, exposure

更年期, menopause

更换、替代, replace

月经, menses

月经, menstruation

月经周期, menstrual cycle

有害的, harmful

有意识的, conscious

有毒 , toxic

有生殖力的, virile

有瘀伤的, bruised

未成熟的，未发育完全的, immature

末端的, terminal

术后, post-op

杀精剂, spermicide

板（滑脱）, disk (slipped)

极度亢奋的, hyperactive

枕, pillow

枪, gun

染色 , stain

标本、（化验的）抽样, specimen

栓剂 , suppository

栓塞, embolism

样本, sample

梅毒 , syphilis

梗阻, obstruction

检查, checkup

检疫, quarantine

植物人狀態的, vegetative

椎间盘突出 , slipped disc

横隔膜, diaphragm

橡皮奶头, pacifier

欣快, euphoria

止痛药, analgesic

止痛药, pain reliever

止血带 , tourniquet

正常/常态, normal

正牙医生, orthodontist

死亡, death

死亡, die

死亡率, mortality

死亡的, dead

死者, deceased

残留物, hangover

残疾, disability

母性/母体, maternal

每日一次的, daily

毒品（通常是非法的）, drugs (usually illicit)

毒液 (蛇、蜘蛛等), venom

毒物, poison

毒素 , toxin

毒血症 , toxemia

毛发 (人体), hair (body)

毛巾 , towel

毛心血管, capillary

气体, gas

气管, trachea

氟化物, fluoride

氣管, windpipe

氧, oxygen

氨, ammonia

氨基酸, amino acid

水, water

水合物；氢氧化物, hydrate

水肿, edema

水蛭, leech

汁，液, juice

汗液, sweat

江湖郎中, folk healer

沙门氏菌, salmonella

治愈, cure

治愈, heal

治疗, remedy

治疗, treatment

治疗, therapy

治疗（动词）, treat

治疗不当, malpractice

治疗师, therapist

泌尿科學, urology

泌尿科醫師, urologist

泡沫, foam

注射, inject

注射 (疫苗等的)、一次注射 (麻醉剂等的), shot

注射器 , syringe

泪（眼）, tear (of the eye)

泵, pump

泻药, laxative

洗涤, wash (to)

洗澡, bath

洗澡（以便）, bathe (to)

活检, biopsy

活的/精力充沛的, live

活着, alive

流产, abortion

流产, miscarriage

流感, flu

流行性感冒, influenza

流行病, epidemic

流鼻涕 , runny nose

测试 , test

海洛因, heroin

海绵 , sponge

涂药器, applicator

消化, digest

消化不良, indigestion

消化系统, digestion

消毒, disinfect

消毒 , sterilize

消毒剂, disinfectant

润滑, lubricate

液体, liquid

淋巴, lymph

淋巴瘤, lymphoma

淋巴结, lymph nodes

淋病, gonorrhea

泪漏, watery eyes

混乱, confusion

混乱的, confused

清醒的 , sober

渗透, penetrate

温度 , temperature

温度计 , thermometer

温柔的；柔软的；, tender

渴望, craving

渴望（成为）, thirsty (to be)

湿疹, eczema

溺水, drowning

滑 、（健康状况等）变差, slip

滑囊炎, bursitis

滑石粉；爽身粉 , talcum powder

滥用, abuse

滴剂, drops

滴管 , dropper

潮热, hot flashes

溃疡, ulcer

潴留、保留、 滞留, retention

激光疗法, laser treatment

灌肠剂, enema

火, fire

灵活, flexible

炎症, inflammation

炭疽, anthrax

烟、吸烟 , smoke

烟草, tobacco

烧伤, burn

烧灼, cauterize

烫伤 , scald

焦虑, anxiety

爬行, crawl

父本, paternal

片剂；药片, tablet

片状, flake

牙关紧闭症, lockjaw

牙痛 , toothache

牙科医生, dentist

牙齿 , tooth

牙齿的, dental

牙龈, gums

牙龈炎, gingivitis

牵引 , traction

狂犬病, rabies

狼疮, lupus

猩红热 , scarlet fever

理疗, physical therapy

瓣膜(瓣) , valve

瓶, bottle

生命/生活, life

生命徵象, vital signs

生命的, vital

生存 , survive

生殖、繁殖, reproduce

生殖、繁殖, reproduction

生殖器官, genitals

生活方式, lifestyle

生物的, biological

生病的, sick

用于固定断骨等的）夹板（名词）, splint (n)

用夹板固定（断肢等）（动词）, splint (v)

用左手的/左撇子, left-handed

甲基苯丙胺, methamphetamine

甲状腺 , thyroid gland

甲状腺机能亢进, hyperthyroidism

甲状腺机能减退, hypothyroidism

甲状腺肿大, goiter

电处死, electrocution

男性/雄性, male

畸形, deformity

畸形, malformation

畸形的, deformed

疝气；脱肠, hernia

疝痛, colic

疟疾, malaria

疣, wart

疤痕 , scar

疥疮 , scabies

疫苗, vaccine

疫苗接种, inoculation

疱疹, herpes

疲倦, weary

疲劳, fatigue

疼痛, ache

疼痛, hurt

疼痛, pain

疼痛的, painful

疾病, disease

疾病, ill

疾病, sickness

疾病；生病, illness

病历, medical record

病毒, virus

病灶, lesion

病理医生, pathologist

症状 , symptom

痉挛、抽搐 , spasm

痒，痒病, itch

痛、疼痛的, sore

痛性痉挛（经期的）, cramps (menstrual)

痛苦的, distressed

痛风, gout

痢疾, dysentery

痣, mole

痤疮, acne

痰, phlegm

痰 , sputum

痴呆, dementia

瘀伤, bruise

瘦 , skinny

瘫痪, paralyzed

瘸子, cripple

瘸的, crippled

癌, carcinoma

癌症, cancer

癌的, cancerous

癔病, hysteria

癫痫, epilepsy

癫痫发作、突然发作, seizures

白内障, cataract

白喉, diphtheria

白血球, white blood cells

白血病, leukemia

百日咳, pertussis

百日咳, whooping cough (pertussis)

皮炎, dermatitis

皮疹, rash

皮肤 , skin

皮肤科医师, dermatologist

盆, basin

盐 , salt

盐水 , saline

监护仪/监查员, monitor

直升机, helicopter

直肠, rectum

眉毛, eyebrow

真菌, fungus

眨眼, blink

眩晕, dizziness

眩晕症, fainting spells

眩晕的, dizzy

眩晕, vertigo

眼睑, eyelid

眼睛, eye

眼科医生, ophthalmologist

眼镜, glasses

着凉（疾病）, cold (illness)

睡眠、睡觉, sleep

睫毛, eyelash

睾丸, testicles

睾酮, testosterone

瞳孔, pupil

矫形外科医生, osteoarthritis

破伤风；强直, tetanus

破碎的, broken

破裂, break

破裂, rupture

硝酸甘油, nitroglycerine

硬化, hardening

硬膜外的, epidural

碎片, splinter

碘，碘酒, iodine

碳水化合物, carbohydrate

磅, pound

磨碎, grind

磷, phosphorus

社会工作者, social worker

祛斑, freckle

祛痰作用, expectorant

神志正常, sanity

神志正常的, sane

神经, nerve

神经学/神经科, neurology

神经官能症, neurosis

神经性/紧张, nervous

神经病学家, neurologist

神经病患者, neurotic

神经痛, neuralgia

禁戒, abstinence

秃头, baldness

秃头的, bald

称重, weigh

移植 , transplant

移植物, graft

稀释, dilute

程序, procedure

空气, air

穿刺针/针头, needle

穿孔, perforation

突变, mutation

窒息, asphyxia

窒息 , suffocation

窒息而死, strangle

窦 , sinus

童年, childhood

笑气, laughing gas

管 , tube

类固醇 , steroid

粉剂, powder

粘液, mucous

粪便, feces

精子 , sperm

精液 , semen

精神/头脑/心理, mind

精神分裂症 , schizophrenia

精神失常；精神错乱, insanity

精神疾病, mental illness

精神病, psychosis

精神病性, psychotic

精神科医生, psychiatrist

糖尿病, diabetes

糖浆 , syrup

紊乱, disorder

紧张型, catatonic

維他命、維生素, vitamin

紧急, urgent

纤维, fiber

纱布, gauze

纹身 , tattoo

组织 , tissue

组织缺氧；氧不足, hypoxia

细菌, bacteria

终止, discontinue

结果 , result

结痂、痂, scab

结肠, colon

结肠炎, colitis

结肠造口术, colostomy

结肠镜检查, colonoscopy

结膜, conjunctiva

结膜炎, conjunctivitis

结论, concussion

绝经前, premenopausal

绝经后, postmenopausal

绦虫 , tapeworm

绷带, bandage

综合征 , syndrome

缓和、减轻 **(痛苦等的)**, relief

缝合 , suture

缝线；缝针, stitches

缺乏, deficiency

羊膜囊, amniotic sac

羊膜穿刺术, amniocentesis

美沙酮, methadone

老年医学, geriatric

老年的、衰老的, senile

耳（中）, ear (middle)

耳（内）, ear (inner)

耳（外）, ear (outer)

耳垂, earlobe

耳塞, earplugs

耳痛, earache

耳聋, deafness

耳鸣 , tinnitus

聋哑者, deaf-mute

聋的, deaf

声带, vocal cord

肉毒杆菌中毒, botulism

肉瘤 , sarcoma

肋骨 , rib

肌肉, muscle

肌腱 , tendon

肌腱炎 , tendinitis

肌萎缩性脊髓侧索硬化症, amyotrophic lateral sclerosis

肘, elbow

肚子, belly

肚脐, bellybutton

肚脐, navel

肛肠科医生, proctologist

肛门, anus

肝炎, hepatitis

肝硬化, cirrhosis

肝脏, liver

肠, bowel

肠, intestine

肠道, gut

股四头肌, quadriceps

股癣, jock itch

股骨, femur

肢, limb

肤色, complexion

肥皂 , soap

肥胖, obese

肥胖症, obesity

肩 , shoulder

肩胛骨 , shoulder blade

肱二头肌, biceps

肺, lungs

肺, pulmonary

肺气肿, pulmonary emphysema

肺水肿, pulmonary edema

肺炎, pneumonia

肺结核 , tuberculosis

肾上腺素, adrenaline

肾功能衰竭, kidney failure

肾功能衰竭 , renal failure

肾结石, kidney stones

肾脏, kidney

肿 , swollen

肿块, bump

肿块, lump

肿块切除术, lumpectomy

肿瘤 , tumor

肿瘤学, oncology

肿瘤科医生, oncologist

肿胀, distend

肿胀 , swelling

胃 , stomach

胃溃疡, gastric ulcer

胃灼热, heartburn

胃炎, gastritis

胃痛/痛 , stomach ache/pain

胃肠病学家, gastroenterologist

胃肠胀气, flatulence

胃肠道 (GI), gastrointestinal (GI)

胆, bile

胆囊, gall bladder

胆固醇, cholesterol

胆红素, bilirubin

胆结石, gallstones

胎儿, fetus

胎儿监护仪, fetal monitor

胎盘, placenta

胎记, birthmark

胚胎, embryo

胚芽, germ

胞衣, afterbirth

胫骨 , shin

胰岛素, insulin

胰腺, pancreas

胶原蛋白, collagen

胶囊, capsule

胸部, chest

胸部 , thorax

胸骨, breastbone

胸骨 , sternum

脂肪 (人体), fat (person)

脂肪 (食物), fat (food)

脉动, pulsating

脉搏, pulse

脊柱 , spinal column

脊柱侧凸, scoliosis

脊柱裂 , spina bifida

脊椎, backbone

脊椎指压治疗师, chiropractor

脊椎骨, vertebrae

脊髓, spinal cord

脊髓灰质炎, polio

脑叶切除术, lobotomy

脑炎, encephalitis

脑膜炎, meningitis

脓, pus

脓疱, blister

脓肿, abscess

脚, foot

脚后跟，踵, heel

脚底（脚的）, sole (of foot)

脚癣, athlete's foot

脚趾, toe

脱水, dehydration

脱臼, dislocation

脸, face

脸朝上, face up

脸朝下, face down

脸颊, cheek

脾, spleen

腋窝, arm pit

腓（小腿肚）, calf (of leg)

腭, palate

腭裂, cleft palate

腮腺炎, mumps

腰部, waist

腹泻, diarrhea

腹股沟, groin

腹腔镜检查, laparoscopy

腹部, abdomen

腹部的, abdominal

腺, gland

腿筋, hamstring

腿部, leg

膀胱, bladder

膝盖, knee

膝盖骨, kneecap

膨大, enlargement

臀部, buttock

臀部, hip

脐带, umbilical cord

自杀 , suicide

自然/天然/固有, natural

自闭症, autism

致命, fatal

致癌的, carcinogenic

舌, tongue

舒适的, comfortable

良性的, benign

色盲, color-blindness

色素减退, depigmentation

节疤, knot

花粉, pollen

苍白, pale

苍白, paleness

苏醒, awake

苦味的, bitter

草药, herb

草药医生, herbalist

荨麻疹, hives

药品/**医药**, medicine

药学, pharmacy

药师, pharmacist

药片, pill

药物/药物治疗, medication

药物依赖, drug addiction

荷尔蒙, 激素, hormone

荷尔蒙的, hormonal

萃取, extraction

萎缩, atrophy

营养, nourishment

营养不良, dystrophy

营养不良, malnutrition

营养品/营养作用/营养/营养学, nutrition

营养学家, dietitian

营养学家, nutriotionist

营养物/营养的, nutrient

葡萄糖, glucose

蓇葖果, follicle

虚弱, weakness

虚弱的, weak

虱子, lice

蛇咬伤 （尤指毒蛇咬的）, snakebite

蛋白, protein

蛔蟲, worms (intestinal)

蜘蛛咬伤 , spider bite

螨, mite

血亲相奸，乱伦, incest

血友病, hemophilia

血块, clot

血小板, platelets

血栓 , thrombosis

血浆, plasma

血液, blood

血清 , serum

血管成形术, angioplasty

血管的, vascular

血管造影, angiogram

血糖过低；低血糖症, hypoglycemia

血糖过高症, hyperglycemia

血红素, hemoglobin

血肿, hematoma

行为, behavior

衣原体, chlamydia

表格, form

表皮, cuticle

衰弱的, emaciated

衰竭, exhaustion

衰老 , senility

衰退, deterioration

被污染的, contaminated

裂隙, fissure

裸露的, naked

视力, vision

规模、天平、鳞屑、鳞片 , scale

视力, eyesight

视力, sight

视网膜 , retina

解剖, anatomy

解毒药, antidote

解释, explain

触摸 , touch

警告, warning

计划生育, family planning

诊察, examine

诊所, clinic

诊断, diagnose

诊断, diagnosis

诊视器、窥镜, speculum

语言, language

语言病理学家 , speech pathologist

诱导，感应, induce

诵读困难, dyslexia

谵妄, delirium

谵妄的, delirious

贪食症, bulimia

贪食的, bulimic

贫血, anemia

贫血的, anemic

贾第鞭毛虫, giardia

起搏器, pacemaker

超声波图, sonogram

超重, overweight

超音波, ultrasound

足医, podiatrist

跌倒, fall

跛行, lame extremity

跟踪, trace

躁狂, mania

躁郁症, manic-depressive

身体, body

輪椅, wheel chair

輸精管切除術, vasectomy

转移病变/扩散, metastasis

轮床, gurney

软膏, ointment

软骨, cartilage

输卵管, Fallopian tubes

输血, transfusion

过敏, allergy

过敏性的, anaphylactic

过敏症, hypersensitivity

过敏的, allergic

过氧化氢, hydrogen peroxide

过量, overdose

过高热, hyperthermia

近视, myopia

近视眼, nearsightedness

进补 , tonic

进食, feed

迟钝的（疼痛）, dull (pain)

透析, dialysis

遗传, genetic

遗传, heredity

遗传的, hereditary

避孕, contraception

避孕套, condom

酊剂 , tincture

酏剂, elixir

酒精中毒, alcoholism

酗酒者, drunk

酶, enzyme

酸, acid

醋胺酚 , acetaminophen

醒來, wake up

采（用）, adopt (to)

重建, reconstruct

重病特别护理, intensive care

重要器官, vital organ

钙, calcium

钙化的, calcified

钠 , sodium

钡, barium

钩虫；十二指肠虫；十二指肠病, hookworm

钾, potassium

铁, iron

银 , sliver

银屑病, psoriasis

铸模, cast

链球菌 , strep

锁骨, collarbone

锤子, hammer

锭剂, lozenges

锻炼, exercise

镇静剂 , tranquilizers

镇静的、镇静剂, sedative

镊子；小钳子 , tweezers

闭塞, occlusion

闭经, amenorrhea

闻 、气味, smell

阉割, castration

阑尾切除术, appendectomy

阑尾炎, appendicitis

阳萎, impotence

阴囊 , scrotum

阴毛, pubic hair

阴茎, penis

阴蒂, clitoris

阴虱寄生病, crabs

阻生齿, impacted tooth

降低体温, hypothermia

除颤器 , defibrillator

陰道, vagina

陰道炎, vaginitis

陰道的, vaginal

隆鼻 , rhinoplasty

隔膜, septum

雌激素, estrogen

震颤 , tremors

霍乱, cholera

青光眼, glaucoma

青春期, adolescence

青春期, puberty

青霉素, penicillin

静脉输液, intravenous fluids

静音/哑, mute

靜脈曲張, varicose vein

靜脈曲張, vein

面筋, gluten

面罩, mask

韧带, ligament

顺势疗法, homeopathy

预后, prognosis

预约, appointment

预防, prevent

预防, prevention

颅骨, cranium

颅骨, skull

颈背, nape

颈部, neck

频率, frequency

颚；下巴；颌, jaw

额头, forehead

颤动, fibrillation

颤抖, shakes

风湿热 , rheumatic fever

风湿病 , rheumatism

风疹 , rubella

风险 , risk

食品, food

食欲, appetite

食管, esophagus

饥饿, starvation

饮食, diet

饱嗝, burp

香烟, cigarette

马镫, stirrup

驼背, hunchback

验光师, optometrist

骨关节炎, osteopath

骨折, fracture

骨板(头颅的), table

骨架, skeleton

骨盘, pelvis

骨科, orthopedics

骨科医生, orthopedist

骨质疏松症, osteoporosis

骨骼, bone

體重, weight

體重變化, weight change

高度，身高, height

高血压, high blood pressure

高血压, hypertension

鳞片状, scaly

鸡痘, chicken pox

鸡皮疙瘩, goose bumps

鸡眼（胼胝）, corn (callus)

麻木, numbness

麻烦, trouble

麻疹, measles

麻痹, paralysis

麻醉, anesthesia

麻醉师, anesthesiologist

麻醉药（合法的）, drugs (legal)

麻醉药/麻醉性, narcotic

麻风病, leprosy

黄疸, jaundice

黑头, blackheads

黑素瘤, melanoma

鼓膜, eardrum

鼠疫, plague

鼻, nose

鼻塞, stuffy nose

鼻孔, nostril

鼻窦炎, sinusitis

ABOUT THE AUTHOR

For more than 25 years, José Luis Leyva has been a translator and interpreter in various technical areas, including the healthcare industry. His vast experience in bilingualism has allowed him to interpret for Presidents, Latin American and US governors, ambassadors, CEO's, judges, prosecutors, forensic experts and healthcare professionals. He is also the author of other books, including technical terminology books of specialized industries.

www.ingramcontent.com/pod-product-compliance
Lightning Source LLC
Chambersburg PA
CBHW070141290526
45789CB00002B/574